STORY OF STEVE THE BETTA FISH

DIYA VS

For my parents and friends

CONTENTS

In the loving memory of Steve, I miss you!

AUTHOR'S NOTE

This book is a tribute to my pet Steve, a betta fish. Before him, I had many other betta fish and I kept them all in our main fish tank. But the fish were eaten and pecked at by my Carp and other fishes. Once, my mother found a betta fish dead in the gravel while she was cleaning the tank. None of them survived for a few weeks. Since I chose to keep Steve in the fish bowl, away from the other fish, he survived for a whole year. I was emotionally attached to him.

He responded to our actions. I used to play with him by moving a key chain, which was shaped like a fish, along the sides of his bowl and he used to move with it. When I put the four pellets of food I gave him every day, he hid at the bottom of the bowl. Only after I gave him all the pellets he swam like a torpedo to eat. I cried a lot on the day he died. That morning I woke up and when I went to the living room, I saw his body on the bottom of the bowl. His fins were completely gone. He no longer looked beautiful like when we first got him. His body was black. I soon found out the pain and suffering bettas go through their life in captivity. I was heartbroken.

I felt that there must be an end to this. Why do people have to cause suffering of other animals? I never knew why. I found out more information about bettas to satisfy my curiosity.

Bettas do have a right to freedom. People ignore it and act as the rulers of the world. After reading the biography of my pet fish Steve, I hope you readers have a better understanding of the challenges betta fish have to face and overcome.

Diya

Hi, my name is Steve and this is my story.

I remember the day that I came to existence in this world. I could remember that there were bubbles surrounding me. I was supported by the bubble nest build by my father. He was supporting the precariously suspended brothers and sisters of me in the bubble nest. He was repairing the nest by blowing bubbles. He also collected the falling eggs from the bottom and deposited carefully into the bubble nest. He already chased away my mother as she was eating the eggs. She was collected from the breeding tank by the shop owner and was deposited into a separate tank. Had she not been removed from the tank, my father would have killed her. I stayed in the bubble nest for three days till I absorbed all the contents of the egg. The egg also contains the food for us, the babies.

I started swimming for the first time. Oh! That was cool. For a few weeks I was breathing the dissolved air in the water through my gills. After about 2-3 weeks I developed the labyrinth organ which allows us to breathe the atmospheric oxygen at the water surface. I was feeding the food pellets that were given by the staff of the betta fish farm. After a month I was separated from my siblings and was kept in a small plastic bag.

One day I was taken to a pet store called 'Happy Family Pets' for sale. I, along with other bettas was transported in a big, crowded box in a blue solution. I only remember falling into the solution. Later I found that it was a tranquilizer to make the fish inactive during transportation.

The people of the pet store were wrong to give that name 'Happy Family Pets' to the shop, because the mood there was not at all 'Happy'. They never let me swim in water; I was confined to a plastic bag and kept in a tank. Though I was inside the tank, the plastic bag did not allow me to swim. The tank had several other differently coloured bettas too in separate plastic covers. I could hardly move in my bag. The pet stores always keep the Betta Fish in small plastic bags as they are easy to sell. Hence more and more Betta Fish get stuffed into the tiny plastic covers and containers.

Few weeks passed. Deep down in my mind I wanted to escape this claustrophobic place and I was counting on the days for my freedom.

Then one day, I saw a pair of twinkling eyes scanning my tank. I met an angel. She was a giant compared to me. But she was scared of the big Labrador dog in the store. With her little finger, she pointed to me and said "I want this fish". Finally there was freedom! I was excited that the family bought me.

Soon, I arrived at their home. I heard them talk about a betta fish that they earlier put in their main tank. Betta fish can survive only with the bottom feeding fish.

It was scared of the goldfish and carp. It dug a burrow in the gravel and stayed there. The food pellets were dropped on the surface of the tank and it could not feed and it died of starvation. So they decided to put me in a fish bowl.

First they washed and cleaned the big fish bowl. They filled it with water and put two strange liquids in the water. One of the liquids was chlorine remover. Chlorine is a disinfectant, which is mixed with the water which people drink, before it reaches their houses. It kills germs in the water that could make people sick. But chlorine makes us (the fish) weak or even kills us. Chlorine can cause chlorine burns, stress and an increase in ammonia levels. Ammonia is toxic to fish. Chlorine burns cause the gills of fish to have a burning sensation. The pain and damage on the fish can cause stress. Stress makes fish vulnerable to disease. Luckily they added the chlorine remover in the correct dose. It did not cause any irritation to me. The other liquid was a fungus remover. Some fungi can cause diseases in fish that could possibly kill the fish. The girl opened my cover and I was released into the bowl. I felt like being liberated and swimming in a big tank even though it was a bowl. I was given enough food at my new home. I started to like it.

One day, I heard a knock at the door. I was wondering who it was. My owner, the little girl opened the door. It was her grandfather. "Hello Ammu! How are you?" Her grandfather asked. "I am fine grandpa; come, let me introduce you to my new friend, Steve". Oh! She gave me the name Steve! She brought him to my bowl. She said "Grandpa, Steve is a boy. The boys are colourful. The girls are dull coloured.""Where did betta fish originate?" He asked. "The betta fish originated in the region of Vietnam,

Malaysia, Thailand and Cambodia. In their natural habitat, bettas live in the rice fields, ponds and slow moving streams" she replied. "How long do they live?" He asked. The little girl took her tab and searched it. She found out that betta fish live up to five years of age in captivity. "Do they come in only one colour?" her grandpa asked. "The betta fish come in red, blue, turquoise, orange, yellow, cellophane, white opaque, copper, black and there are multicolour varieties too", she replied. Bettas have different types of tail too. Some of the tail types are Veil, Crown tail, Half-moon, Delta, Super Delta, Double, Spade, Fan, Rose, Plakat, Combat and Comb tail.'

Different Tail Types in Betta Fish

Comb Tail

Crown Tail

Double Tail

Half Moon

Plakat Tail

Rose Tail

Combat tail

Super Delta tail

Her grandfather told her that he too liked fishes and many of the fishes that were very common in his childhood are slowly disappearing from the natural water bodies.

By the time their dialogue finished, it was bedtime. My owner switched off the light and went to bed. Suddenly I saw a lizard on the brim of my bowl. I was scared. I thought it was going to eat me. I swam to the bottom of the bowl in fear. Luckily my owner's father came to get a glass of water to drink. He saw the lizard and shooed it away. He placed a wire mesh over my bowl to stop any lizard from entering my bowl.

The next morning my owner put a plant in my bowl. I felt exhausted as I can only breathe at the surface of the water. There is a misconception that betta fish feed on the water plants. We are natural insectivores and feed on mosquito larvae. Mosquitoes spread many harmful diseases among humans. So the betta fish are beneficial to humans.

I told you earlier, I lived with my siblings in a huge tank with our dad. All bettas need a big tank. But people do not care for them. They keep us in tiny vases or bowls with dirty water. They even keep us in cups. Only a few people take care of their pets like my owner.

My siblings may be suffering in some other part of the world. Like us, many fish are not taken care of properly around the world.

Betta Fish in a small plastic bag   **Betta Fish during transport**

Betta Fish kept in a cup with dirty water

My mind was filled with thoughts of how betta fish suffer. When we bettas are kept in cups there is a high ammonia build up. Ammonia can kill fish. Ammonia is developed from the excretory waste. We cannot swim around freely at all in the small cups. We are prone to diseases when we are kept in such conditions. Bettas need their water to be free of poop. We should be fed with enough food. The suffering is heartbreaking. But it is still a common practice today. Why should I be sad for myself? All those bettas suffering out there, what can I do? Nothing!

The little girl asked her parents about their love of fishes and about their experience with fishes. Her father told that in his childhood, there were plenty of fishes in streams and ponds near to his house. The water was more clear and free of pollutants at that time. Her father had to cross tiny streams on his way to his school. He said that in the morning sun he could see many small fishes glistening in the water. He and his brother used to catch those fishes using bathing towels without any bait. After trapping the fishes in the bathing towel, they released the fishes back to the stream. He used to feed the fishes in the stream with broken pieces of ground nut. He felt happy to see the fish closer when they surface for feeding. He did not know that fishes are kept in aquariums at homes till he saw an aquarium in one of his relative's house. There were gourami, guppy, goldfish and angel fish in the aquarium. He said that it was fun to clean the aquarium and replacing the water in the aquarium. Worms were dugout from the area near the well and were fed to the fish. Lucky fish, I am bored of the feed pellets!, I thought.

The fish were also given broken pieces of boiled rice. He and his brother used to visit their grandparents on summer vacation. The grandparents lived on the bank of an irrigation canal. During summer, the dam will be open and water from the dam is used to irrigate the land.

Once the dam was open and the canal started to flow, the water was diverted to basins of the coconut palms. The water filled one basin and then flowed to the next basin and so on. While observing the water flowing on their land, the girl's father noticed a few dark figures moving in the water. Using a bucket, he trapped the swimming creatures. They were found to be Tilapia, a fish that is endemic to Africa and it became an invasive fish in Kerala. It was grown for edible purposes. After keeping the fish in the bucket for some time, he found that the fish stopped swimming and were surfacing. His uncle told him that there is no air in the water and hence they are coming to the surface. Oh! This is the reason why there are aerator pumps in aquariums. They released the fish back to the stream.

The girl's father also told that he was once terrified by a fish. One day when he woke up, he saw a gunny bag in the kitchen. His mother told that there are fish in the bag. One of his uncles caught the fish during the previous night. His uncle dumped the gunny bag onto the kitchen floor. They were huge Indian mottled eel. They can grow up to 1.2 meter in length and 6 kilogram in weight. He was terrified of the sight for no reason! Yes, there are even bigger and scary fish among fresh water fish. A few can cause serious injuries to humans like the Piranha.

Few days later the little girl's grandmother came for a visit. She was very happy to see me. She asked my owner, the little girl "your betta fish is looking lonely. Why you did not put another betta fish with him?" She replied "when you keep two male bettas together they fight with each other over their territory. Sometimes they shred the fins of the opponent to pieces."Some people keep two male bettas together. This results in many fierce conflicts. We are also known as Siamese fighting fish due to this. Some people keep bright coloured fish with bettas. If the colourful fish are the same size of the betta, the betta may attack. Males should be given a chance to mate with females and produce healthy offspring. Female betta fish can be kept together. Male betta fish can be kept with dull coloured fish to prevent conflict. Keep male and female bettas together only for breeding. They may have conflict too. Bettas should not be kept in vases or a glass that may let the fish jump out of the water.

The little girl's mother was also very much fond of fishes. She had a collection of her own when she was a kid. She wanted to have her own aquarium tank, but her father disapproved. But she decided to build her own tank. She collected few bricks, sand and some cement and attempted to make a tank. Seeing this, an elder man from the neighborhood helped her and a small fish tank of three bricks tall was constructed. Some boys near her home used to breed guppy fish during the summer vacations and used to earn money by selling them. She bought her first fish from one of those boys. They were a pair of guppies. They were called 'Sari Vaalan' locally which translates to Sari Tail. This means that the tail is shaped like Sari, a traditional dress of Indian women. There was a male and a female. Guppy males are attractive and have a colourful tail. The females are dull coloured. After some time the tummy of the female started bulging out. Guessing that the female was pregnant, she was transported to a new glass jar and was kept in the dining table so as to get more attention. One day, the little girl's mother found lot of fries swimming in the water. After some time all the fries disappeared. The mother guppy ate all of her babies. Later she was moved to the main tank. A few aquatic plants were added to the tank. Probably the plants served as hiding places for the guppy fries. The water in the tank was replaced periodically to keep the fishes healthy. For this, first the fishes were kept in a mug and then released back into the tank after refilling with clean water. One day, during the tank cleaning, the little girl's great grandfather thought that the mug was containing just water and emptied it to the ground. All the fishes started jumping up and down gasping for air. It was a tense moment for the little girl's mother. Immediately, she collected the fish and put them back into the mug with water. The fish were fed live worms and rice. There were no pests and parasite attack during those days.

One day my owner's friend came for a visit. After seeing me, she asked for the fish food. My owner showed her the fish food. She took it and ran towards my bowl. She had taken a huge scoop of food. My owner told her not to do it. But it was too late. She had put the fish food in the bowl. The bowl was full of red and green pellets. My owner's mom saw what had happened and changed the water in the bowl. Good thing! She saw it.

Over feeding usually causes a bloated stomach, swim bladder disease and constipation in bettas. It also makes the tank or bowl water dirty. This results in the growth of microbes too.

After changing the water, my owner's friend asked "After your betta fish lays eggs and when they hatch, give me the betta fish babies." "No I cannot give you the babies."My owner replied. "Why?"Her friend asked. "My betta fish is a male. He cannot lay eggs."She said. "But how will you breed them if you have a male and a female?"Her friend asked with enthusiasm. "To breed bettas you must first learn about their breeding habits and how many eggs they can lay. Prepare a breeding tank for the bettas. Find a young pair of female and male bettas. Let the bettas adjust to the tank. So it is best to buy them early, about a few months from breeding. Put a temporary divider in the tank. Feed live food to the bettas during breeding. Raise live food for the betta fry. Put the bettas in. Put the female on one side of the divider and the male on the other side. Watch their behavior and look for any signs of conflict. Remove the divider when the male is ready to breed. Let the fish breed. The female will start laying eggs. The eggs will fall down and usually both the male and female will swim down to collect the eggs and to blow them into the bubble nest. Remove the female after egg-laying. Keep the male in the tank until the fry can swim. Feed the fry with live food like baby brine shrimp and micro worms. Move the fry to a bigger tank when they grow".

Male Betta and the fries in the bubble nest

Brine shrimp (the feed given to the fries)

On hearing this I recollected the memories of my journey in which I was in that horrible tiny plastic bag underneath all the other bettas in the box. The horrible journey lasted for several days.

The next morning my owner's father was doing some photography experiments. He was taking pictures of my little owner. She asked him to take photos of me. He wiped all the dust on the outside of my bowl in order to get good photos. With his camera he took many photos of me. My owner took my photos every single day on her mother's mobile phone.

A few weeks later, tragedy struck. I fell victim to a disease called fin rot. My fins were ragged and turned black. They were not beautiful as earlier. I was treated with a medicine called 'Potassium permanganate'. It comes in the forms of small granules and need to be dissolved in water before applying to the fish tank. I was in good condition for a few months after the treatment.

Many people also do not bother to find out what type of disease a betta fish has. People who keep betta fish should be aware of the diseases of betta fish and the pathogens that cause them. There are many diseases that can affect betta fish such as fin rot, tail rot, ich, fungal infections, popeye, advanced fin and body rot, velvet, dropsy (pine coning) and swim bladder disorder. Ich is a disease caused by a protozoan. It damages the gills and skin of the fish. It causes white spots on the fish. Popeye causes the eyes of the fish to bulge outwards.

Fin rot

Fungal disease

Velvet disease

Swim bladder disease

Dropsy

Fish Ich

Major diseases of betta fish

Dropsy is a symptom of bacterial and parasitic infections. It could also mean the fish has liver disease. Regular water checks should be done to check if a betta fish is sick.

For a few glorious months, I was better than ever. I enjoyed my life as a betta fish. Nothing interfered with my happiness. But one day I felt sick. I again had fin rot. My owner was shocked to see a sudden come back of the disease. They tried their best to save me. But I could not hold on to good health.

One day, I felt very weak. I could not swim at all. My owner observed me for many hours with tears in her eyes. As the hours passed by I lost my fins and I sank to the bottom of the bowl. I could not move to the top to feed on the fish feed pellets given by her. She even tapped on the sides of the bowl to check if I was alright. She was very upset and so were the other family members. Few more hours passed by and my vision got blurred and I bid good bye to the wonderful world...

Did you know?

- Bettas are listed vulnerable by the International Union for Conservation of Nature (IUCN).

- Bettas are probably the second most popular fish kept, after Goldfish.

- Bettas can be found in standing waters of canals, rice fields and floodplains in its natives(Mekong basin   of Thailand, Laos, Cambodia, and Vietnam)

- Most of the bettas die young just because they are kept in bad conditions in stores.

- Betta fish fighting is a common sport in Thailand.

- The betta got its name from an ancient clan of warriors, called the "Bettah." The fish were given a combatant name after the fighting fish became popular in the mid-1800s.

- Bettas are very aggressive. If you hold a mirror near to it, it will think its reflection as another betta and will make an attacking pose.

- They may also become aggressive towards other tropical fish with large fins such as guppies, angelfish and others.

- Bettas collected from the wild are dull brown and green with red on their fins. Their fins are much smaller. Breeders create bolder and brighter betta colours, patterns and shapes by selective breeding.

- Bettas exhibit strong sexual dimorphism. Male bettas are typically larger than females and display brighter colours with more attractive fins. As a result, the vast majority of bettas kept as pets are male.

- Bettas are intelligent and can be trained. They can recognize their owners. Some people even train their bettas to perform simple tricks, like following their fingers around a bowl or swimming through hoops.

- Betta fish are becoming rare in the wild. But when they escape from fish farms they become invasive species.

- In January 2014, a large population of betta fish was discovered in the Adelaide River Floodplain in the Northern Territory, Australia.

- In 2017, a man in Connecticut was sentenced to 20 days in prison for killing a Betta Fish!

- In Singapore a man was fined 2500 Singapore Dollars for operating an unlicensed Betta fish store in the year 2017!

- Male Betta fish make bubble nests only if your tank or bowl has suitable conditions.

- Some female bettas make nests too.

- Bettas are species of the Gourami family.

- The first betta fish in Europe were royal pets.

- The natural habitat of the betta fish has little dissolved oxygen. So they have adapted to breathe atmospheric air and considered as a labyrinth fish which has the unique ability to breathe oxygen directly from the air and also take in oxygen from water through its gills.

- Unique parental care is exhibited by male bettas. Betta fish are raised by their dads. The male chases the female away right after laying her eggs.

- The scientific name of the ornamental betta fish is *Betta splendens*. *Betta* means 'enduring fish'and *Splendens* means 'shining'.

- Every betta fish has a personality and aggression level.

- Bettas can grow up to 7.6 cm in length.

- The betta is known as "plakad" in its native Thailand and has often been referred to as "The Jewel of the Orient."

- The myth that betta fish fight to the death is not true. The injuries the betta fish along with diseases caused by stress may kill the fish.

- Bettas have upturned mouths and primarily feed from the water surface.

- A good diet for betta consists of dried bloodworms, brine shrimp or daphnia. Commercial betta food or pellets combines all three foods, in addition to vitamins and minerals.

- On an average betta fish live up to 2 years in the wild whereas it can live up to 3 years in captivity. Maximum life span is 5 years in captivity.

- A betta fish's bite force is stronger than a great white shark. However the human skin is strong enough to withstand a betta bite.

- Betta fish are carnivores in the wild. They feed on insects and their larvae.

- The marble betta was created by a prison inmate named Orville Gulley. He raised bettas in his peanut butter jars. He was trying to create a black butterfly betta but instead discovered the marble gene.

- The most expensive betta in the world is coloured like the national flag of Thailand and costs $1500 USD.

Source https://asiancorrespondent.com

New words for young readers

- Black Moor – a variety of goldfish also called Black Telescope

- Bloat- become swollen with fluid or gas

- Brine shrimp- tiny creatures in water

- Carnivore – an animal that feeds on other animals

- Claustrophobic- Fear of   small and closed places

- Conflict – a serious argument, quarrel or disagreement

- Disinfectant- a chemical that destroys germs

- Endemic- restricted to a certain place

- Fry- fish babies

- Gasping-to breathe loudly and with difficulty, trying to get more air

- Gills- the respiratory organ of aquatic animals like fish

- Glistening- shine with a sparkling light

- Insectivore - a plant or animal that eats insects.

- Invasive- spread in a quick or aggressive manner

- Irrigation- the supply of water to crops

- Lifespan – the length of time for which a person or animal lives

- Pathogen – a microorganism that can cause diseases

- Pollutants - substances that make air, water, soil *etc* dangerously dirty

- Poop - waste product from an animal's digestive tract

- Potassium permanganate – a purplish coloured crystalline solid, which is used by aquarists for the disinfection of plants and aquarium components. It is used to remove organic build-up in tank water, and kill bacteria and fungi that infect fish.

- Precariously - likely to fall or collapse

- Protozoan – a single celled microscopic animal of the Kingdom Protista eg. amoeba

- Surfacing-rise or come up to the surface of the water

- Tranquilizer - a substance that induces sedation.

- Territory -An area defended by an animal or group of animals against others of the same sex or species

- Vulnerable- in danger

Made in United States
North Haven, CT
29 March 2023

34695201R00028